D1257844

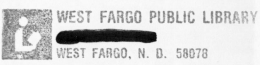

FINDING A
COMMON LANGUAGE
CHILDREN LIVING WITH DEAFNESS

DON'T
TURN
AWAY

For a free color catalog describing Gareth Stevens' list of high-quality children's books call 1-800-433-0942.

Library of Congress Cataloging-in-Publication Data

Bergman, Thomas, 1947-
       Finding a common language

       (Don't turn away)
       Summary: Follows the activities of a six-year-old Swedish girl as she attends a nursery school for the deaf.
       1. Children, Deaf--Juvenile literature. [1. Deaf. 2. Sign language. 3. Physically handicapped] I. Title. II. Series: Bergman, Thomas, 1947-   Don't turn away.
HV2392.B47   1989   362.4'2'088054   88-42969
ISBN 1-55532-916-0

D O N 'T
T U R N
A W A Y

North American edition first published in 1989 by

Gareth Stevens, Inc.
7317 West Green Tree Road
Milwaukee, Wisconsin 53223, USA

First published in Swedish in 1987 by Rabén and Sjögren under the title *Som du och jag*.

Copyright © 1989 this format, by Gareth Stevens, Inc.
Photographs and original text copyright © 1987 by Thomas Bergman
Additional text and design copyright © 1989 by Gareth Stevens, Inc.

Series Editor: MaryLee Knowlton
Research Editor: Scott Enk
Series Designer: Kate Kriege

Printed in the United States of America

1 2 3 4 5 6 7 8 9 95 94 93 92 91 90 89

FINDING A
COMMON LANGUAGE
CHILDREN LIVING WITH DEAFNESS

DON'T
TURN
AWAY

Thomas Bergman

Gareth Stevens Children's Books
MILWAUKEE

When Thomas Bergman first showed me the remarkable photographs that appear in Finding a Common Language, I was struck by their power to capture the essence of children's personalities and moods. As we looked at them together — I for the first time, he once again after many times — I was moved by the intensity and passion of a person who cares deeply about children who are deaf.

Thomas is Sweden's best-known children's photographer, with a reputation stretching from Europe to Japan. His compassion, admiration, and affection for children with disabilities inspired him to embark on a special photographic mission. The striking black-and-white photographs you will see in this book will remain in your memory. The thoughts and feelings that Thomas' young friends have shared with him form the basis for the insightful text that accompanies the pictures.

You will meet children in the pages of this book with a disability that may be unfamiliar to you. You will be inspired by the originality and courage with which they meet the challenges presented by this disability. And you will be moved by the many ways that they are like children everywhere. I hope you will ask yourself, as I did, "Why haven't I met many children like these? Where are they? Why don't I see them in the schools and on playgrounds, in museums and shopping malls, on the streets and in the parks?" These are the questions we must explore. Our communities should embrace all people. We will _all_ be the richer for it.

In Finding a Common Language, Caroline and Marcus show us that a disability should not be a cause for embarrassment, separation, and fear. Instead, it should be a reason for reaching out, sharing the joys, sorrows, and hopes of our lives.

Gareth Stevens
Gareth Stevens
PUBLISHER

Meet Caroline, who is six years old. Everyone calls her Lina. Like many other six-year-old girls, Lina likes the color pink. Pale pink, dark pink, hot pink — you name it, Lina loves it! Even her shoes are pink. Lina was born deaf in her left ear and almost deaf in her right ear.

Lina has a brother, Marcus, who is nine years old and also deaf. Their parents have normal hearing. The children and their parents communicate with sign language and speech reading.

On weekday mornings, Lina takes a taxi to a special school for children
with hearing impairments. She has attended this school since she was
a tiny child. She is part of a group of ten children who primarily "talk"
with their hands, using a special language called sign language. This is
Lina's last year here. Next year she will attend first grade at a school for
deaf children.

The morning begins with a fuss. As usual, Lina doesn't want to wear her seat belt. When she was smaller, the seat belt always crept up around her neck. Her mother points out to her that she's older now and the seat belt fits fine. She also tells her that she's old enough not to make such a fuss. But she knows Lina fusses a lot these days because she's worried about leaving her old school. By the time she gets to school, her bad mood is gone and she greets her friends and teacher with a smile.

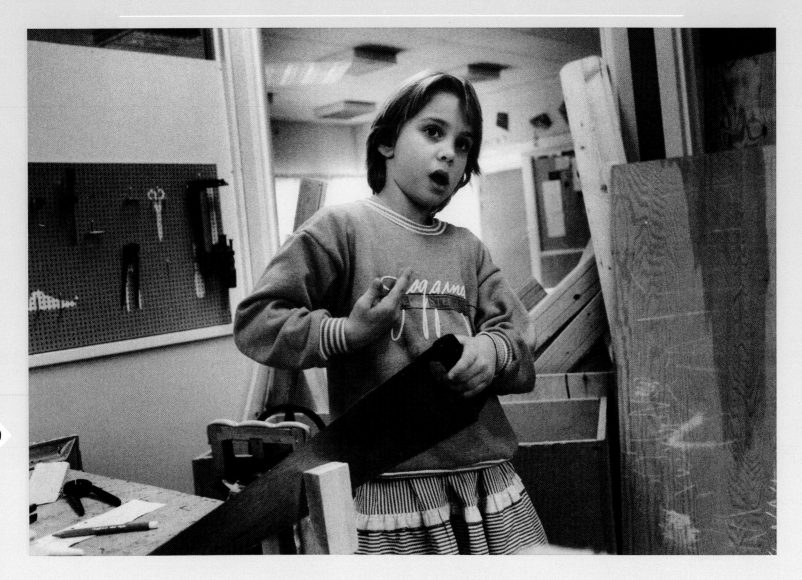

The children and the teachers start the day by discussing what they will do.
Lina decides to build an airplane out of wood. The teacher tells Lina
to start with a drawing — a plan. But Lina doesn't want to do a drawing.
She wants to go right to the wood. She has a plan in her head already.

Lina picks out a long piece of wood and saws it in two. With a hammer and nails, she attaches the wing. Finally she fastens two wooden wheels to the body of the plane. Tomorrow she will paint it. Tonight she'll make another plan in her head for the color scheme.

It's Lina's turn to set the table for lunch. With her friend Axel, she gets the plates, glasses, and silverware and puts them at each place. When everybody is at the table, the soup is brought out. The children take just a little soup because they know they will have a special dessert today.

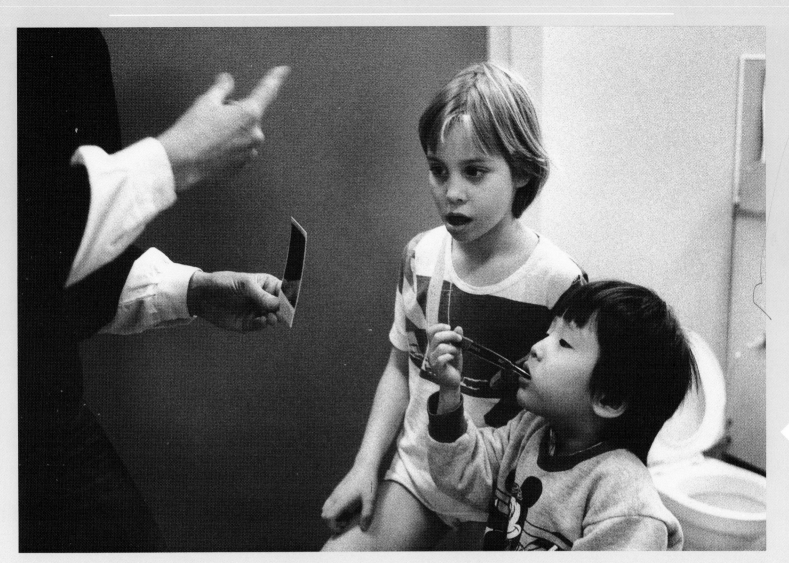

The children talk a lot at lunch. Lina and her friend Sandra have secrets to share. They duck their heads under the table and sign excitedly to each other. You can't whisper in sign language, so they have to sign so that no one else can see.

After lunch all the children brush their teeth and wash up. Axel has a new soap that his grandmother sent him. Everybody has to smell it. It smells like roses. The teacher takes a picture of the children crowding around Axel and his rose soap. Axel isn't so sure he wants to smell like a rose, but he likes the attention.

Lina and her friends gather in the reading corner for a story. Today's story is *The Wild Baby*, everyone's favorite. The children sit spellbound as the teacher's hands tell them the story of a baby girl who can do everything, swing from a light, climb in a garbage can — in short, what all children would love to do.

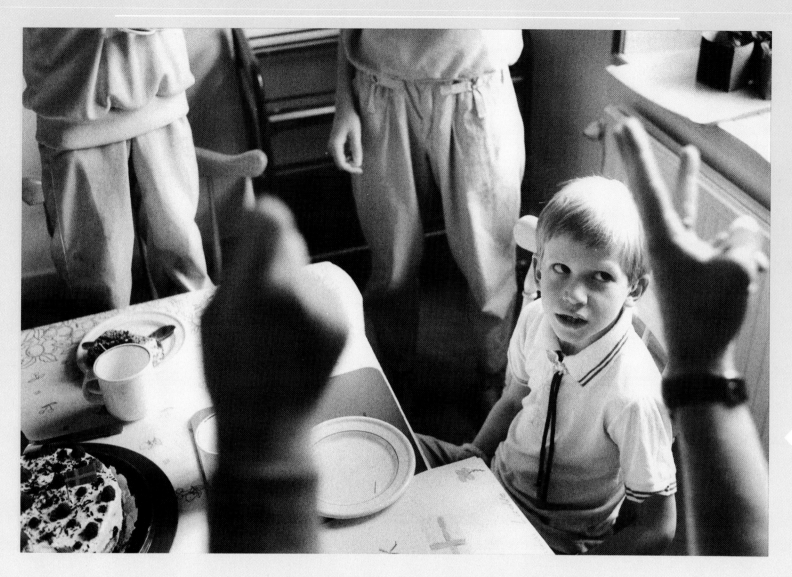

Today is Frederick's birthday. Everyone sings "Happy Birthday" to him, using sign language, of course. Now for the cake!

While the smaller children nap, Lina and the other six-year-olds have a lesson. The teachers are preparing them for the school they will attend the next year. Today the girls are so giggly that the teacher finally gives up and tells them to make a picture for Frederick because it's his birthday. Lina draws a big red heart with "Lina loves Frederick" inside. She hides the picture from Sandra, who has drawn two children kissing. Under the children it says "Sandra loves Frederick."

The children and their teachers use every way they can to communicate with each other. Some of the children can't hear anything. Some, like Lina, can hear a tiny bit, maybe just high sounds or low sounds. Others can hear a little but the sound is distorted and doesn't sound the way most of us are used to hearing it.

The teacher has hung a microphone around Lina's neck. When Lina speaks into it, the other children can hear her at listening stations around the room. The microphone broadcasts only Lina's voice to each of the listening stations. None of the classroom noise is picked up, so it's easier to hear Lina talking.

When it's Mikaela's turn to speak, Lina makes faces because she doesn't think her speaking sounds good. Learning to speak is not easy when you can't hear yourself very well or at all. The children help each other with whatever hearing they have . . .

. . . though not always in the nicest way.

The class is conducting a bake sale. First they have to bake the cookies. Lina decorates hers — all in pink, of course — lavishing special artistry on a porcupine cookie. The other children make their cookies, big and small, in every color of the rainbow. Everyone except Lina agrees that the turquoise ones are the finest.

After baking the cookies, the children make a sign for their bake shop and play money to pay for their cookies. Then they place the cookies on trays on the counter. Lina tends the shop. She tells the children to line up, and soon all the cookies are sold — except the pink porcupine. Lina has refused to sell it at any price. It goes home in her book bag.

Today Lina and her mother are at the hospital for a hearing test. The therapist has told them that she's running late. Lina signs that she wants to get some candy from the vending machine. Her mother signs back that it's okay and gives her some money. Lina has been here often to be tested and fitted for devices that will make the best use of what hearing she has. She knows her way around.

Lina's hearing aids are designed especially to meet her needs. Everyone's hearing loss is different. Some devices work better for some people than they do for others. Some work better in some situations than in others, too. Lina's hearing aids work best when the room is quiet except for the one person or thing she needs to hear. Her hearing aids make everything louder, so if there is too much background noise, she has trouble sorting out the sounds. The technician has made a mold of her ear on which she will base the shape of the new hearing aid.

Lina knows the testing routine very well. Out of Lina's sight, the therapist makes sounds with a machine. She starts with quiet tones and increases the volume. Lina puts a wooden ring on a peg every time she hears a tone. She can hear only the deep, dark tones. The bright, high tones don't register in her ears.

Based on the results of the test, the therapist picks out a new hearing aid. Because Lina's auditory nerve is damaged, no hearing aid can make her hear perfectly. It can only help her to hear some sounds better. This one makes the noises and rattling so much louder, too, that Lina doesn't want to wear it. Lina's mother and therapist know that if the hearing aid bothers Lina, she will take it off whenever she can, so they decide to look for something more suitable.

Sometimes parents don't know that their children are not hearing well until the children start school. By that time, they have missed out on a lot that goes on around them. Children who may have hearing problems are those who are not talking by the time they are a year old, or those who often don't come when they are called, or those who talk louder than other children. These children should have their hearing checked by a doctor or a school nurse.

Today Lina and her classmates are going to the Silent Theater. Here deaf actors are presenting a fairy tale about a magic pearl. The play is about a poor orphan boy named Bau who lives in a country ruled by a wealthy and cruel emperor. One day a bird tells Bau about a magic pearl that makes all wishes come true. After a long search, Bau finds the pearl, only to have it stolen from him by the emperor. Bau gets the pearl back with the help of his animal friends. The play ends with Bau promising to use the pearl to grant only good wishes. The children are still and thoughtful after the play ends. They usually accept their hearing losses, but today each one has a wish for the magic pearl.

After the production, the children are invited up onto the stage to meet the actors. Hands fly with questions as they try on the masks. Lina starts thinking about a theatrical career. "And why not?" answer the actors when she asks them about it. "It's a fine life!"

Every Tuesday, Lina and the other six-year-olds in her class attend the Manilla School, where they will go next year. Here Lina meets her future classmates. The day is tightly packed with plans. The children begin by sitting in a circle telling each other about their weekend. Later they will do some work in an exercise book. In the afternoon, they spend time with special friends from the next class who will show them around and take care of them when they come to school full time next year.

Lina's teacher is John. John's hearing is normal. He talks to the children, using sign language as he speaks. This way the children have three ways of understanding him: they can read the signs, they can read his lips, and those with some hearing can hear some of what he says.

Friday is show-and-tell day. The children are eager to show what they've brought from home. Lina shows them her new doll. Everybody gets to hold it and cuddle it. The class names the doll Eva. Frederick has brought a pair of weird glasses. Axel thinks they're terrific and wants to keep them. After a tickling match, Frederick gets them back.

Today, some children from another day-care center have come to visit Lina's school. These children are not deaf. Lina and her classmates are going to teach them a song using sign language. The smiles and hugs of the children are part of a universal language, a kind of speaking everyone uses. Often, children who are deaf prefer to be with each other. But when the deaf and hearing children learn to communicate, they feel comfortable together. Too often, however, only the deaf children make the effort — and they grow tired of it.

It's spring! The children are too squirmy to be kept inside all day, so the class is going on a picnic. They are thrilled to be outdoors with their backpacks filled with lunches. They cross a meadow where cows and newborn calves look up drowsily. Both Frederick and Axel just happen to step in cow pies, of course. Lina and Sandra have brought a jar with holes in the lid. They are going to catch small insects and feed them grass.

From the edge of a small pond, the teacher waves to the children. She holds out her loosely closed hand. The children are wild with delight as she opens it to reveal a tiny frog. As they jabber with their hands about where they'll keep it and what they'll feed it, the frog jumps back into the pond.

This doesn't get the children down. They happily move on to the next event — lunch! The sandwiches and chocolate milk are delicious in the fresh air. The children eat quickly so they can go back to their fun.

The children are dancing butterflies today. They begin as sleeping butterflies, waking to music from four vibration boxes standing on the floor. The music comes out of the boxes as vibrations instead of sounds. When the teacher turns on the tape recorder, the children feel vibrations in their bodies. The butterflies wake up one at a time and dance.

Lina plays with a smaller boy, Ola. As he sits on one of the vibration boxes, she surprises him by talking loudly into the microphone. He feels the vibrations. They tickle and he giggles.

The small children play a game called "Grampa in the Box" with a drum. Mindy is the Grampa. The teacher hits the drum five times. Mindy feels the vibration and counts to five and stands.

34

Lina has had a hard day. She started out in a bad mood, and things got worse. She and Mikaela had a bad fight, hitting each other and pulling each other's hair. The teacher made them stop, and Lina was angry because she was blamed for the whole mess. She told the teacher that Mikaela was calling her names with signs. But the sign language is hard and the children and grown-ups don't always understand each other very well.

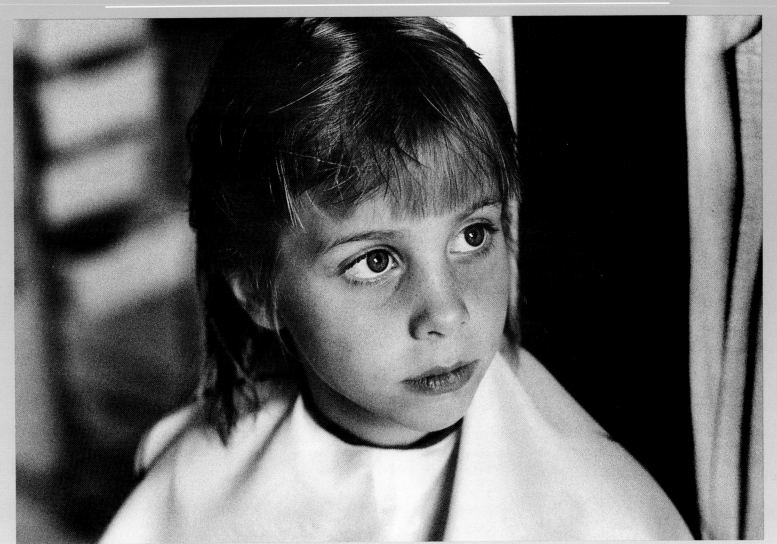

After school, Lina's mother takes her to the hairdresser. Lina signs that she just wants a trim. She doesn't want to look like a boy. After summer vacation, Lina will start at her new school. She is very happy about that. She is too old for day care and is bored with it. All she can think of is the Manilla School. She is looking forward to having new friends who know sign language and wants to be with older children she can learn from.

Lina is going with Mikaela and her mother to a swimming pool today. Mikaela comes here twice a week for a kind of physical therapy called adaptive aquatics. It is mostly water exercises. Today is the last day of the semester, so she can bring a friend.

The girls hurry through the dressing room, changing into their swimming suits and showering before they enter the pool. Mikaela shows Lina some of her exercise movements. Because it's the last day, the therapist lets Mikaela do just what she wants, and the hour passes quickly as the girls play with the ball.

Did you know that your ears do more than just hear? The system that makes you hear is also responsible for balancing your body. Some kinds of hearing loss also result in a loss of balance. The physical therapy that Mikaela receives has taught her ways to compensate for the shortcomings of her inner ear.

Mikaela and Lina are sorry to leave the water. But they hurry as they shower and dress again so they'll have time for an ice cream cone before they go home.

The light on the wall is flashing. That means the phone is ringing. It's Mike, calling for Marcus. Since neither Marcus nor Lina can hear on a regular phone, the family has a special text telephone. It's like a typewriter with a TV screen or a personal computer.

"Hello, Marcus," Mike writes. "What should we do tomorrow?"
"Let's play soccer," Marcus answers. Marcus can't write too fast yet, but he's learning. Lina will be learning to read next year. Then she can use the phone, too. It's a wonderful device for communicating. If ever Lina or Marcus needed help, they could call the police or fire department.

38

Having an older brother like Marcus has been great for Lina. He taught her to ride a bike. Now that it's spring, they ride every spare minute. Mostly they ride on paths and small roads near their house. Their parents don't want them riding on main roads because they can't hear the cars. They can see what's in front of them but they have no way to tell what's behind them or out of their vision to the left or right. But both children are determined to go where they want and they ride on the main road anyway.

40

When she's not at school, Lina plays with hearing children. Her friends are redheaded sisters, Silvia and Helena. Silvia is Lina's very best friend. Lina has taught her sign language. As Lina gets older and her language ability increases, she will teach Silvia more. Helena has learned by watching Lina and Silvia.

Lina is a strong-willed girl. She knows what she wants to do and how to do it. But she becomes frustrated often because she has such a hard time making herself understood. Being misunderstood makes her very angry. She is good with sign language and will, of course, get better. But this is not just her responsibility. Hearing people must also learn to understand and communicate.

QUESTIONS FROM CHILDREN ABOUT DEAFNESS

When we try to imagine what it would be like to be blind, we can close our eyes and know what we're missing. But we can't think in the same way about being deaf because we always hear something, even when we're sleeping. Our hearing connects us to the world and helps us, in ways we are not aware of, to learn language and to think. Here are some answers to questions you might have had about hearing and hearing loss.

What does it mean to be deaf?
It means that even with a hearing aid, a person cannot understand spoken conversation. The person may hear some sounds, but the sounds are not loud enough or precise enough to be relied upon. Many people now use the term "hearing-impaired" because the word "deaf" causes so many misunderstandings. Both are still used, though.

What do deaf or hearing-impaired people hear?
Everybody's hearing is different. But there are two basic types of hearing loss, or hearing impairment: a decibel loss or a frequency loss. A decibel loss means that *everything* a person hears is quieter than it would be for a person with normal hearing. A frequency loss means that *some sounds* are quieter to the person than others. Usually, a person with a frequency loss misses the high tones.

What causes deafness?
Hearing loss and deafness can be caused before birth by problems in pregnancy. A pregnant woman who catches German measles, for example, may have a child with hearing problems. Diseases such as meningitis can also cause deafness by damaging the nerves of the inner ear. Exposure to loud noises such as music (even through headphones), gunfire, and factory sounds can cause hearing loss, too. This type of hearing loss can show up years after the person is exposed to the damaging noise.

Are deaf people also mute, unable to speak?
Physically, deaf people are like people with normal hearing; some are physically able to talk while others are not. But there may be other reasons that they do not talk.

Hearing people learn to talk because they hear the sounds other people make and they try to make those sounds themselves. They learn the speech patterns and language of the talkers around them. Deaf people cannot hear other people talk and they cannot hear themselves talk. This makes learning to speak extremely difficult. With therapy and very hard work, many deaf people learn to talk. But usually their pronunciation and voice do not sound exactly like those of a hearing person.

People with hearing impairments are aware of the reactions of people who can hear them speak. They may prefer not to speak at all to avoid being stared at or ridiculed.

If they cannot hear, how do deaf people learn to speak?
Deaf people learn to speak by watching and by touching. For example, a little deaf girl cannot hear what her therapist says or what she herself says. So she uses other clues.

Here is an example. As the therapist says a word, the girl puts her fingers to his lips to feel the tension and the passage of air. She touches his throat and chest to feel the vibrations there. She watches his face carefully as he forms the sounds of the letters. Then she says the word herself, looking in the mirror. She feels her own lips, chest, and throat to duplicate what she felt and saw when the therapist spoke. The therapist tells her if the sound is good. They work at it until she can duplicate the sound.

At home and at school, deaf children may be able to use a computer to improve their speech. In one system the children choose a word. They type it into the computer. The correct pronunciation of the word appears on the screen. The children then say the word into a microphone hooked up to the computer. Their pronunciation appears on the screen. The children compare the two patterns and work to make them the same. Many deaf children like the independence the computer gives them.

Why don't people with hearing losses wear their hearing aids all the time?

Most hearing aids make everything louder. In a setting with a lot of background noise, like a play-room or a party, turning up the volume on all sounds is not helpful. The person wearing the hearing aid will have a hard time sorting out the sounds and their meanings. Many people can hear some sounds, such as low tones, fairly well. But the hearing aid makes these sounds louder for them, too. This can be painful.

Why do some people seem to hear better at some times than at others?

What a person with a hearing loss is able to hear can depend on the other noises in a room. Too much background noise can interfere with a hearing aid or distort other sounds.

Something else is very important here, too, though: What people seem to hear may not be what they are hearing at all. What they understand includes what they take in through their other senses. People who have experienced a hearing loss learn to compensate by paying attention to other things around them. For example, such things as facial expressions, the reactions of others who are listening, and hand gestures provide information that hearing people may not have to rely on. If the lighting is not good or if the speaker's face is hidden, these sources of information are not there. This kind of "listening" takes a great deal of concentration. A tired person may not have the energy to pay attention in so many ways and will not seem to "hear" as well.

Can deaf people use the phone?

Yes. For many years deaf people have been able to use a TDD, which stands for Telecommunications Device for the Deaf. But this only works if the person sending the message and the person receiving it have a system. Mainly deaf people, government offices, and libraries have these systems. A person using this phone types a message that is printed out on the receiver's machine.

Technologists have made TDDs more flexible in recent years. Some can communicate with other TDDs, computers, and fax machines; a fax machine works like a photocopying machine, but instead of merely photocopying a message, it sends the message over the telephone wires to its destination.

SIGNING

How does signing work?

When signing, people communicate by using their hands to represent what others say with their mouths and hear through their ears. The two basic types of sign language are Exact English and American Sign Language (Ameslan). Many people learn to use both, along with speech reading, to give themselves as much chance to communicate as possible.

With Ameslan, gestures represent words, phrases, and whole sentences. It does not use the grammar of English, so it is rather like "speaking" a foreign language. It works well for deaf people when they communicate with other deaf people. Hearing people can also use it with deaf people, but because sign language has many limitations, they will probably not be able to express everything they think.

THE AMESLAN SYSTEM

Here are some signs from the Ameslan system.

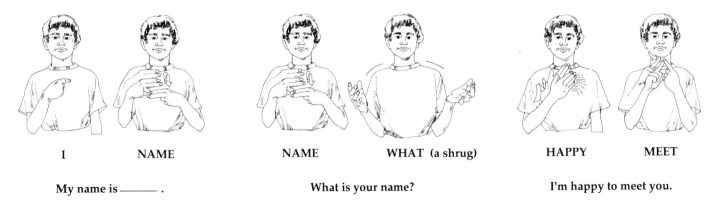

I   NAME   NAME   WHAT (a shrug)   HAPPY   MEET

My name is ———— .   What is your name?   I'm happy to meet you.

EXACT ENGLISH SIGN-LANGUAGE SYSTEM

Exact English is a sign-language system that uses English sentence structure and grammar. Children who learn this system think and communicate in the same language hearing people use. Here is the alphabet.

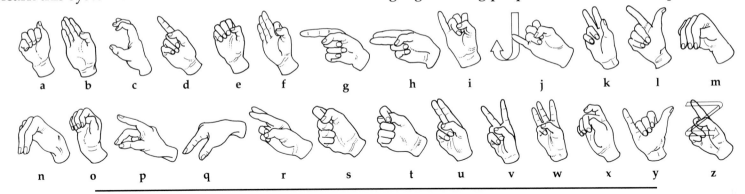

a   b   c   d   e   f   g   h   i   j   k   l   m

n   o   p   q   r   s   t   u   v   w   x   y   z

. . . MORE QUESTIONS

How do deaf people communicate with people who can't sign?
They work with a trained interpreter. Interpreters are paid professionals who can sign and speak. Most people do not have their own interpreters. They call an agency of interpreters and make arrangements as they need to. This can be inconvenient because interpreters are not always available. Many deaf people rely on someone close to them for much of their communication with people who do not know signs. They also write their messages.

How does speech reading work?
Speech reading is a method of figuring out what people are saying by watching their faces, especially their mouths, as they speak. Many hearing people think this is the best way for deaf people to "hear" others. But it cannot tell a deaf person everything someone is saying. On the lips, half the sounds in English look like at least one other sound. And many sounds formed inside the mouth and throat cannot be seen or "read." A very good speech reader can understand only about half of what is being said.

Do people who have never heard think the same way we do?
Young children who have been deaf since birth do have some difficulty understanding the language of abstract ideas.

For example, a little deaf boy can understand a sign or even a speech-read word for "dog" when you draw or point to a dog. And he will learn that "juice" can be signed for or spoken if you give him juice when he requests it. "Let's go upstairs," can be conveyed through signs, gestures, and movements toward the stairs. But "We'll go upstairs after you finish your juice" is more complicated. This is because the concept of time is an abstract idea, and understanding abstract language is very difficult for a child who has not heard language.

In order to increase a child's understanding of the purpose of language and the process of speaking, most people now feel that the deaf child — as well as family, friends, and teachers — should use every means of communication they can. Parents of deaf children learn signing from the time the deafness is discovered. They both sign and speak to their children.

How can I help people who speech-read understand what I am saying?
You can face them when you speak to them. Don't turn your face away — even when you're not talking — because they won't know they are missing something. Speak normally, neither more loudly nor more slowly than usual. People who speech-read have learned to read normal speech and if you distort the volume or speed of your speech, you will not produce the movements they have learned to expect. Keep your hands away from your face and don't talk with food in your mouth.

How can hearing and hearing-impaired people improve their communication?
More than any other disability, deafness isolates people from each other unnecessarily. Deaf people and hearing people must break the sound barrier. Hearing people must become familiar with and accept the unusual sounds of deaf people's speech. We must speak with greater care. We must learn the signs of their languages. We must be patient and willing to try new ways of communicating, to learn from each other. This is the responsibility of people who can hear as well as those who cannot. It takes two to communicate, and both must work at it when it becomes difficult.

45

THINGS TO DO AND TALK ABOUT

Here are simple things to do that will give you some idea of what it is like to have a hearing impairment.

1. See what it is like to have a frequency loss. Write three sentences of about ten words each. Then write them again leaving out the following: *s, sh, ch, t, th, p,* and *f.* Can you figure out the words by reading them? Read them out loud to friends. Can they figure them out? You'll probably find that you can understand some of them but not all. This kind of uncertainty about words is what occurs when a person with a frequency loss receives spoken language.

2. For a few days, look for the letters **cc** or this symbol ♉ at the beginning of TV programs or check your TV listings for these signs. What programs have this sign listed next to them? What programs do not? All in all, how much TV is available for people with hearing problems?

3. See if a technical school or your public school system offers courses in sign language and speech

reading. You might be able to take a course free. Children can learn sign language more easily than adults, and most programs welcome your participation. Take a friend. You can then both learn and practice together.

4. This experiment will give you an idea of some of the difficulties a person would have relying on speech reading for information. If possible, video-tape about ten minutes of an action program or drama. If you can't tape it, turn off the sound. Watch without any sound. How much can you understand of what the actors are saying? Can you figure out what is going on? If you've taped the show, play it back with the sound. How much did you have right?

MORE INFORMATION ABOUT DEAFNESS — PLACES TO WRITE AND PEOPLE TO CALL

The people at the offices listed below will send you information about hearing impairment and deafness if you write to them. Many of them also have state and local branches as well as the national offices listed here. Check your phone book if you want to talk to someone locally. Be sure to tell the people what you're interested in so they can send you the material that will be most useful.

Alexander Graham Bell Association for the Deaf
3417 Volta Place NW
Washington, DC 20007

American Society for Deaf Children
814 Thayer Avenue
Silver Spring, MD 20910

American Speech-Language-Hearing Association
10801 Rockville Pike
Rockville, MD 20852

Council on Education of the Deaf
800 Florida Avenue NE
Washington, DC 20002

Helen Keller Center for Deaf-Blind Youths and Adults
111 Middle Neck Road
Sands Point, NY 11050

National Association of the Deaf
814 Thayer Avenue
Silver Spring, MD 20910

MORE BOOKS ABOUT HEARING, SPEECH, AND DEAFNESS

The books listed below are about children like you who are deaf. Some are fiction and some are about real children who have something to tell you. Look for them in your local bookstores or school and public libraries. If you cannot find them, ask someone to order them for you.

Amy, the Story of a Deaf Child. Walker (Lodestar)
Anna's Silent World. Wolf (Lippincott Jr.)
Belonging. Scott (Gallaudet)
Claire and Emma. Peter (Harper & Row)

Computers for the Disabled. Cattoche (Franklin Watts)
Feeling Free. Sullivan (Addison-Wesley)
Handtalk: An ABC of Finger Spelling and Sign Language. Charlip and Beth (Macmillan)

I Can Sign My ABCs. Chaplin (K. Green)
I Have a Sister, My Sister Is Deaf. Peterson
  (Harper Jr.)
Keeping It Secret. Pollock (Putnam)
The Late Great Dick Hart. Payne (Houghton Mifflin)
Now I Understand. LaMore (Gallaudet)
The Silent One. Cowley (Knopf)

Skipper. Dixon (Atheneum)
The Swing. Hanlon (Bradbury)
We Can. Star (Alexander Graham Bell Association
  for the Deaf)
What Is the Sign for Friend? Greenberg
  (Franklin Watts)
Words In Our Hands. Litchfield (Whitman)

GLOSSARY OF WORDS ABOUT HEARING AND DEAFNESS

Here are some words that will help you understand what it means to be deaf. They will also explain some of the devices and methods people use to adjust to a hearing impairment.

amplify: make louder.

closed captioning: a system, indicated by the letters **cc** or a symbol like this ⧉® on the screen at the beginning of a TV show or videotape, by which people with a special decoder on their TV set can see the spoken words printed along the bottom of the screen.

deaf: unable to understand speech, even with a hearing aid.

decibel: the measuring unit for volume, or loudness; the higher the decibel level, the louder the sound is.

decibel loss: a hearing loss that makes all sound less loud, comparable to turning down the volume on the radio.

finger spelling: making signs with the hands to spell out names and words.

frequency loss: a hearing loss of high or low tones, usually high. Since words are made up of high and low tones, a person with a frequency loss usually hears only parts of words; it is especially difficult to pick up the sounds *s, sh, ch, t, th, p,* and *f.*

hearing aid: a machine that amplifies sound. Deaf people cannot hear speech, but most of them can hear something. So they wear hearing aids to make the most of what they can hear.

hearing-impaired: a term describing a person who hears nothing at all or hears less than a person whose hearing is normal does.

lip reading: see *speech reading.*

mute: unable to speak.

pitch: the quality of a sound; it changes depending upon frequency, loudness, and force.

sign language: a system of communication that uses signs made with hands to convey language.

speech reading: formerly called lip reading; telling what people are saying by watching the shapes their mouths make. A good speech reader can understand about one-half of what is being said in English.

47

INDEX

48